The
Homework Trap

ISBN-10: 061557680X
ISBN-13: 9780615576800
Library of Congress Control Number: 2011944985
CreateSpace, North Charleston, SC
Wyndmoor Press, www.wyndmoorpress.com

Wyndmoor Press
515 Grove Street
Suite 3-D
PO Box 187
Haddon Heights, NJ 08035

Cover design: Meg Schultz, www.megschultz.com
Author's photograph: Steve Sharp, www.stevesharp.net

The
Homework
Trap

~

How to Save the Sanity of Parents, Students, and Teachers

by

Kenneth Goldberg, Ph.D.

Other books by Kenneth Goldberg

Peter Squared (a novel)
Published by MacAdam Cage (2000)

Differing Approaches to Partial Hospitalization (editor)
Published by Jossey Bass (1988)

For my son, BB

ABOUT
THE HOMEWORK TRAP

The bookstores are filled with books about how parents can get their children to do their homework. Finally a book comes along that shows the *student's* perspective, and that actually helps parents understandthe reasons behind their child's persistent homework problems instead of offering the same tired suggestions.

The Homework Trap is truly a breakthrough book for parents and teachers. By sharing his personal experiences as a psychologist and parent of a homework non-compliant child, Goldberg helps parents "get inside their child's head" and gain insight into their child's frustration. He explains why traditional interventions for homework non-compliance from both parents and school can actually create more discouragement and avoidance in the child. It's a huge piece of the "puzzle" of homework non-compliant children.

The Homework Trap not only explains the psychology behind homework non-compliant students, but it gives fresh, practical advice for parents about understanding the power hierarchy of the school system, and how parents can redefine their relationship with teachers. Goldberg helps parents calm the homework battles with their child, and regain control of their child's free time.

An invaluable resource for frustrated parents, *The Homework Trap* offers a thoughtful reexamination of traditional approaches to homework non-compliance. It is written in a conversational, easy to understand style. It should be required reading for all teachers, school counselors, and principals.

Dr. Cathy Vatterott, Author of *Rethinking Homework: Best Practices That Support Diverse Needs*.

Kenneth Goldberg has given us a roadmap for re-thinking how to deal with homework problems in children. Coining the term, the homework-trapped child, Goldberg takes us on a journey through the psychological and learning theory principles that he believes explain the problems that some students face with homework. He argues that between 10 and 25 % of students in school today are homework-trapped. To these students and their parents, Goldberg will become a hero. He debunks the myths about homework non-compliance and replaces these tired assumptions with solid evidence for thinking of homework problems as *educational* problems and not as behavioral or moral problems. For example, he talks about the myth of motivation and how many children are told, "You're so bright, and you could make As if you only tried." Goldberg details how these children can learn at the A level, but they still have difficulty performing at that grade level. According to Goldberg, they also have more difficulty completing their homework than they do completing work they are given in school. Since teachers see the child at school, but not at home, Goldberg argues that they have trouble comprehending just how difficult it is for the child to work at home. Goldberg repositions problems of homework non-compliance as "under the radar" learning problems and goes on to recommend how to work with your child and their school if they are homework-trapped.

Goldberg does not take a stand on whether or not schools should give homework, but rather gives parents tools for helping their homework-trapped student. Much of the book uses learning theory as a way of explaining how the problems for the homework-trapped child compound as they move through school. To me, the most interesting part of this analysis is his discussion of working memory and processing speed, and how these two attributes have a profound impact on a child's ability to do homework.

Goldberg provides guidelines for parents to follow at home, in dealing with the school and the community at large. In terms of the home, Goldberg recommends that parents assume the role of head of the home and to stop letting schools impose dictates on family life. For him, this is important in terms of having the homework-trapped child not see the family as impotent in the face school mandates. Goldberg recommends that parents with homework-trapped children form community groups in order to learn that they are not alone in the homework challenges they face. In the end, it is the school and the teachers who have to come to a new understanding of the challenges that some students face when it comes to homework. By suggesting a term, homework-trapped, and by situating homework problems as 'under the radar' learning problems, Goldberg helps us see that homework problems develop over time and that they are educational problems, NOT moral or behavioral problems. In this way, Goldberg moves the homework debate into some new and important territory. And he also helps the thousands of families who fight each night over homework. Where was this book when my son was growing up?

Dr. Etta Kralovec, Co-author of *The End of Homework: How Homework Disrupts Families, Overburdens Children, and Limits Learning.*

Table of Contents

INTRODUCTION

I n 1901, the California State Legislature passed a law that essentially prohibited teachers from assigning homework to children under high school age. For the next half century, homework played a fairly minor role in education, a practice that changed after Sputnik was launched. In waves, from the space race with Russia to the technology race with Japan to the No Child Left Behind Act, America has successively put increasing pressure on its teachers, and that pressure has filtered down to its students and spilled into their homes (Kralovec, 2007). Are we on the right track? Is this helping our children? Do children learn more now than they did before? Or, as people believed at the start of the twentieth century, does homework actually do more harm than good?

This has been a topic of current debate. Experts argue on both sides of the issue. Some schools have gone far to look at their policies and reexamine the practice (Hu, 2011). Yet, for the most part, homework remains as standard fare, generally accepted and commonly given as an expected component of a child's education.

There are some very good books on the market today that criticize modern homework policy (Bennett and Kalish, 2006;

Kralovec and Buell, 2000; Kohn, 2006; and Vatterott, 2009). There are other books geared to help parents help their children be more successful with homework (Rosemond, 1990; and Dolin, 2010). This book is different. It stems from my personal experiences as a student and a parent, and my professional work as a clinical psychologist. It is geared toward the parent of a homework-noncompliant child, where both parent and child seem hopelessly homework trapped. Frankly, I wish there had been a book like this on the market when my children were growing up.

I don't have strong opinions about whether or not homework should be given. I have doubts about its value, but I believe in deferring educational decisions to those who teach our kids. My concern is not homework, per se, but homework policy and its effects on some kids. I believe that anywhere from 10 percent to 25 percent of all children have such serious problems completing their assignments that, on balance, the overall effect of demanding that they comply does more harm than good. That's my estimate—perhaps it's less, perhaps it's more. But in speaking to countless parents and teachers, the feedback I get is nearly universal. Everyone has a homework horror story to tell. Let me start by explaining my connection to homework and why I felt compelled to write this book.

My memories of homework from my childhood are scant, probably because my parents took a laissez faire attitude when it came to school. For the most part, they left it to my brother and me to deal with our teachers.

Up through fourth grade, I had a very positive school experience. I was an avid reader and gifted in math, so whatever assignments I had coincided with what I thought of as fun. In those early years, I was consistently the top student in my class.

Things changed after fourth grade, when I had an operation. This was 1957, and pediatric heart surgery was in its infant stage. A fair number of children were dying on the table. Although I did not know this at the time or for most of my adult life, oxygen deprivation and some brain trauma could not be avoided with the surgery I had. I came out of the surgery still able to learn and very strong in math, but my ability to read went dramatically downhill. So I could still excel in math, but English, science, and social studies all became difficult, as I could no longer read at a reasonable pace.

My grades suffered so that when I graduated from high school, my grade point average was slightly under a B, and for the first three semesters of college, I ran a mid-C. Then, in the second semester of my second year of college, I made a major decision that turned my grades around. Although I went to school planning to become a doctor, possibly a psychiatrist, I changed directions and majored in math. I took fifty-five math credits when only thirty-six were required for a major, and my grades went up dramatically, as I could ace my courses without having to read. I went on to Columbia University for doctoral studies in mathematics. I excelled and stayed one year before facing a crisis: I did not want to be a mathematician. I dropped out, applied to study psychology, and gained admission to a doctoral program. By then, through a combination of maturation, motivation, and adaptation (i.e., I learned how to skim through books and cull the most important parts), I was able to get by. I did not lack discipline; after all, I've stayed with long-term projects, and I've published my doctoral dissertation, one volume in my field, a literary novel, and this book. My major problem has always been a lack of reading speed. I'm convinced, in retrospect, that my operation caused a severe *under-the-radar* learning disability that did not keep me from learning but affected my schoolwork. It had a greater effect on homework than it had on the work I did in class.

Now, my experiences as a parent: Like my parents, I chose to stay relatively uninvolved with my children's school. My oldest, like me, appeared to do well from the very beginning and went on to surpass me at every stage. He was practically a straight-A student from elementary school through college, and I don't think he ever worked very hard. Like all kids, he liked video games, avoided chores, and was probably lazy at heart. It didn't cause him problems at school. He just did well. Today, he's a hardworking man pursuing a successful career. I don't think he learned to be disciplined. He just pursued what he liked and evolved to where he is now.

My second child had more difficulties. There were many panicked mornings when the homework had not been done. "I need to stay home to finish my homework!" she would cry. We wrote the notes, claiming the proverbial stomach virus, and let her stay home to finish her assignment. She graduated with lower grades in high school than her older brother, but she went on to a college of comparable prestige and proved quite diligent and successful at her work. She is pursuing her career, and, like her older brother, she is quite a hard worker. Frankly, if I compared these two children, I would say that she was the more diligent worker when she was young. It's just that her talents did not lead to doing homework with ease. I'm sure there are other parents who would have made different decisions when faced with her last-minute *"I didn't do my homework"* states. I don't know. Maybe we were wrong, and those parents would have been right. But that's what we did, parenting our children, being who we were.

For our third child, life was very different. From the start of second grade, his unwillingness or inability to do his homework became an issue of crisis proportion. We had numerous parent-teacher conferences, multiple *agreed-upon* plans, and constant battles at home. We tried everything from positive reward to outright nagging. Still, homework dominated our house every day. In effect, my wife and I went *off target* from our basic philosophies of how to raise our children, with daily pressures to get this or that assignment done, always with the warning that if he did not do it now, he would suffer when he got to the upper grades. Ten years of homework terror, and there is not one indication that he benefitted from our efforts in any way.

The essential nature of life is that children are raised by imperfect parents who happen to be, to kids, the "best mommies and daddies in the world." The only thing any of us can do to serve our children well is to be who we are, try to stay real, and love them to death. Our youngest endured *off-centered* parents, driven by a demand to complete all of his assignments that, at least to us, did not make sense. If we had not had him, I wouldn't be writing this book. I'd be stepping back, shrugging my shoulders, and wondering, "What's the problem with homework?" With him, my experiences and attitudes have been radically changed.

Now, let me tell you what I understand through my work as a clinical psychologist. Unlike many of my colleagues in the field of psychology who deal with homework problems, I'm a general psychologist, not a school psychologist or a child psychologist. Whereas those psychologists work with children when they display problems with learning and behavior (e.g., when homework difficulties are dominant), I'm the Paul Harvey of my field. (For those who don't know the reference, Paul Harvey was a legendary radio announcer from Chicago whose hallmark phrase was, "And now, for the rest of the story.") My primary professional perspective comes from my work with adults, not with children, and what happens to people who have long-term homework problems after they grow up. After all, we educate kids to prepare them for the future, so it is important to understand not just what is going on today when we're trying to get them to do their homework, but what the future holds for their adult lives.

In my work, I've met with thousands of disabled adults, years after they've finished school (or not finished school because they've dropped out). Some have always been unable to work. Others have learned to work successfully with their hands as carpenters, plumbers, electricians, and mechanics, despite the fact that they hated school and did poorly there. They are typically men (hence, my use of male pronouns throughout this book) in their forties or fifties, have a physical ailment, perhaps chronic back pain, and have to retrain, if they're going to work. They are terrified at the prospect of going back to school. Their childhood experiences were frighteningly like those of our youngest child. And they could have been helped if the system had been changed, possibly for all, but certainly for them.

This book is written in eight short chapters. Chapter 1 is the Core Problem. Here I will explain how ongoing homework struggles have a cumulatively negative effect for both your child and for you, and why it is important for you and the school to change your approach as early as possible. I will note the preeminence of time as a central notion in understanding homework problems, and why our notions about the task have to be changed. In Chapter 2, I address the Myth of Motivation to explain why the idea that your child is lazy or lacks motivation is simply not true, and why behavioral problems are not the cause of homework resistance, but the outgrowth of constant, unrelenting homework pressures. In Chapter 3, I discuss Behavioral Factors, which support homework noncompliance. Here, I give you a minicourse in behavioral psychology to help you see why the approaches typically used to get a child back on track don't help out. In fact, they add to the problem.

In Chapter 4, I discuss Modeling and Maturation, two critical factors that get overlooked in addressing children's homework problems. In Chapter 5, I discuss the Systems Effect. Here, I'll review the relationships between you, your child, and the school in the context of organizational dynamics. This will help you understand how parent-school homework partnerships create family-school structures, which actually undermine your effectiveness as a parent. In your efforts to get control of your child's behavior, you actually get drawn into a pattern of behaviors that weakens your authority with your own child. The problem may seem complex, but it is worth understanding in order to correct homework problems.

Chapter 6 addresses Learning Issues. Here, I introduce the notions of working memory and processing speed, and how they interfere with homework compliance. I will include special considerations for children with ADHD. In Chapter 7, I'll offer specific recommendations about what you want from the school, and what you can do at home. Chapter 8 will summarize this book.

This is a short book with simple ideas based on complex notions from the science of psychology. It does not present *everything you wanted to know about homework (but were afraid to ask)*, but it will get you started thinking about your child's homework problems in very different ways from what you've been told by the school or read in other books. It will leave you with the task of convincing the school to try a new way to deal with this nagging problem. You may want to give copies of this book to your child's teachers, or contact me directly at www.thehomeworkdoctor.com.

One final note: I offer an acknowledgement to Dr. Jay Kuder, professor of special education at Rowan University. Dr. Kuder and I have spent hours discussing the problem of homework compliance from his perspective as an educator, and from mine as a psychologist. We have presented workshops before parents, teachers, and school psychologists, and, over the years, we have strongly influenced each other's points of view. He has provided me with invaluable insights into the educational aspects of homework problems. Without his influence, I could not have written this book.

1. the CORE PROBLEM

Before you can escape the homework trap, you need to understand it. You may talk with other parents and feel bad, knowing that, even if they complain about homework, their children are moving on. You may have other children of your own who are doing well. It is hard to realize just how brutal this situation can get, until you are homework trapped yourself. The problem feels relentless.

Your child may enter school with great enthusiasm. Before long, he does poorly on his assignments. He may do some work but fail to hand it in. He may do some work, but it takes the whole night, leaving him no time for anything else. Eventually, his efforts stop, his grades go down, and the slide begins.

Whatever the specifics, you are a responsible parent who wants to support the school. You get *the call,* so you go to meet with the teacher. At this point, there are three primary parties involved: You (and your child's other parent), your child, and the teacher. In its simplest form, here is what is happening:

- The teacher assigns and grades the work.

- Your child does not do some or all of the work.

- You feel responsible for your child's behavior.

To visualize what is happening, picture yourself at the fulcrum of a seesaw trying to lever your child up to success, so that he does what he's expected to do.

Elementary School

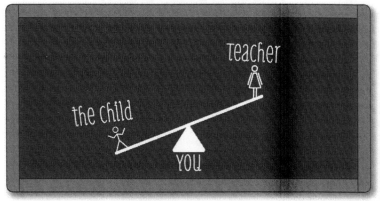

The teacher pushes down (by giving assignments), but the child does not move up. This creates different relationships among you, your child, and the school than would have developed if your child did the work.

Hopefully, you can help your child achieve success, so you can take yourself out of the fulcrum role. If you can't, you'll find yourself constantly feeling like you have to do something for your child to succeed. There are some experts who will tell you to back off and let your child take responsibility for the work himself. This is great advice—if it works. Unfortunately, even those who suggest this approach acknowledge that there are many children for whom this doesn't work.

Soon, your child will have more than one teacher. Your child may act out, so others at the school will start to get involved. The pressure mounts, you feel crushed, and the only thing that stays the same is that your child doesn't do the work.

Upper Elementary School

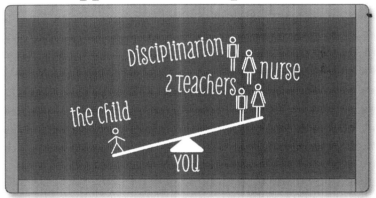

Now, you're feeling panicky and know something has to change. Household tensions, not your child's performance, are what are moving up. There are warnings of trouble ahead in the upper grades.

By middle school, things look like the following:

Middle School

Your child has four or five teachers. Hormones are kicking in, and he's reached an age where peer approval is vitally important. He may be in a larger school with new classmates, whom he did not know before. He looks for acceptance and may find it with children other than the ones he knew from elementary school. He may express his frustrations by acting out, which only brings in a larger cast of characters. You may look for outside help (e.g., a learning center or a child psychologist), hoping that these strategies will turn him around. Meanwhile, your child may feel the pressure but still fails to act. If anything, he may act out against the adults instead of focusing his attention on the work he is required to do. It may seem as if the only thing happening is that you are caving in under the weight of the problem.

Finally, we have this:

High School

In the process of partnering with the school to *solve the problem,* you may become increasingly burdened (crushed in our illustration) and overloaded with meetings, while continuously watching your child decline. If your child plays sports, athletic consequences kick in, which means your child is separated from the activities he loves and the peers he has always had. This becomes particularly devastating since many activities he enjoyed before (such as Little League Baseball) are mostly available through the high school. Athletic ineligibility, based on academic problems exaggerated by homework noncompliance, serves to isolate your child from his peers, and this increases the risk of his dropping out and gravitating to activities you want him to avoid.

Shouldn't the School Know What To Do?

The school is charged with educating your child. Federal law (Individuals with Disabilities Education Act, Public Law 108-446, 108th Congress) mandates an adequate education for all children, including those with special needs. The schools have methods for helping children with learning disabilities. To qualify, your child would have to get classified by a child study team. There are other formal (such as a 504 plan under Section 504 of the Americans with Disabilities Act Amendments Act of 2008) and informal (such as the work of sensitive teachers) means by which a child's special learning needs can be met.

Unfortunately, schools have only the perceptions and solutions they have. If a problem is perceived as one of misbehavior, then the solution will entail a behavioral-management plan. If teachers see it as a learning problem, then they'll look for an educational solution. Even then, much will depend on the approaches they have. It is my strong belief that the majority of children with chronic homework problems have *under-the-radar* learning problems, requiring solutions I have seen only in my own work. Consequently, much depends on how well you can *educate* the teachers to think a different way.

In early elementary school, you have the benefit of dealing directly with one teacher. If the teacher is willing and has administrative support, you have some flexibility to try new ideas. As your child grows up, the number of people involved grows. Each person will have different ideas about what your child needs. Some may be willing to change. Some may not.

Although the school works as a team and may come to some agreement, not everyone may concur with the result. Academic independence is a longstanding principle, and this may collide with the collective agreements formed when you and a group of educators meet. As a result, it's not always certain that decisions will be carried through. Obviously, this differs from school to school and school district to school district. In some places, the school administration or child study team has great power. In others, the decisions you and they make may not get enforced. Even if the law is on your side, your child's experience is based on what happens in his classroom day by day. Frankly, you're not looking to battle schools. You're looking for solutions that not only serve your child but also make things easier on the school.

With the number of classrooms increasing as your child gets older, there is always a risk that nothing will change in a class or two. Add athletic consequences to the unsolved problem, and a well-designed plan may fall apart. Your child may even feel like he is trying, but he will give up if he is excluded from his favorite sport. He may do better in many of his classes, but what if one teacher does not agree to reduce the workload, piles on homework, and gives your child a failing grade? Your child feels deceived, and he no longer goes along.

By the end of this book, you will see that I have a specific model for how to approach your child's homework problem. Although I have many ideas that will unfold as you move through this book, there is one concept that is so important, and potentially so controversial, that I'll share it with you now. That's the following issue:

Time

The school day starts and stops by the clock. Perhaps your child's school runs from 9:00 to 3:00. There's a bell to tell him when school starts. There's a bell to tell him when he is dismissed. His day may be divided into specific instructional periods, which also start and stop at the sound of a bell.

Homework is an assigned volume of work. Although the teacher (and the district) may have some time standards in mind, there is no bell to let your child know when homework time starts and (more importantly) when homework time stops. Those time standards are estimates, at best, and generally pertain to the "average" student.

Children work at varying paces for different reasons. The faster a child works, the less homework (measured by the clock) he has. Children who are particularly adept may have no homework at all, since they often finish their assignments in class, before they leave school (possibly while waiting for your son to finish his work).

I believe that many homework problems would stop if homework were redefined as a standard of time, rather than as a volume of work. I consider time-based work a reasonable accommodation for homework-trapped children. Instead of requiring that your child complete all of his work, regardless of how long it takes, I recommend requiring that your child do all the work that he can in a set period of time. Frankly, I think this is a worthy idea for school districts to employ for all children as well.

I understand that this recommendation will seem radical when considering common practices in education today. A shift to a truly time-based standard would alter the parent-teacher partnership, since schools would have to rely on parents as their source of information to confirm that the child did what he was told to do. It would create modifications in the grading system, since children would not be penalized for work they did not do, as long as they worked for the required amount of time. In the end, this suggestion might cause educators to rethink (without necessarily abandoning) the role homework plays in the teaching process.

I do not oppose a policy that gives children work to do at home. I take no position on what types of assignments teachers ought to give out. I respect that these are professional issues for educators to work out among themselves in their field. I simply consider it essential that children have a time-limited workday, in class and at home.

The Risks at Hand

I understand that implementing my ideas, time boundaries in particular, may be hard to do. Yet, I encourage you to take this on, as your child's long-term growth and development may depend on getting this right. There are real problems, which can emerge later on, caused by homework pressures, which teachers and school psychologists never get to see.

With a negative high school experience, which is an ultimate outcome of chronic homework problems, your child may have little drive to keep moving on. Teenagers are moody to begin with, and constant negativity does not help. And it does not help to just lay the blame on your child, since the result is the same: His future is compromised.

There is actually both good news and bad news for homework-trapped children, when they grow up. The good news is that maturation is on your side. Your child will eventually become an adult and be in charge of his life. If he has skills (say, works well with his hands), he may do well. Good moral values and his ease with people may carry him through to the next stage of life.

The bad news is that adolescence is a risk-taking time. Healthy teenagers take chances. If your child has hope, he'll generally put limits on the risks he takes. If he does not, he may do things (involving sex, alcohol, drugs, joyriding, criminal activities, or suicide) that compromise his future.

Over the years, an ongoing diet of critical responses for not doing his work has a cumulative effect on how a child sees himself. If he does not see a future, he'll take more risks.

2. the MYTH of MOTIVATION

"**Y**ou're so bright. You'd be an A student, if you just tried harder," your child's teacher says, as she gives him one more lecture on doing his work. She shrugs and thinks, "It's a shame. He's just not *motivated.*"

Motivation is a word that gets bandied about often when we look at the problem of homework compliance. Those other students are motivated. Yours is not. If he just got motivated, he'd do so well.

Whether stated or not, the motivational hypothesis is strongly ingrained in the ways in which we commonly address homework problems. In most school systems, there is an expectation that children will do homework. The teacher may have a formula by which homework is scored and factored in. There may be points-off for work that is late and zeros for work not done at all. The child may stay in for lunch or recess, or he may get afterschool or weekend detention. Some of these penalties seem geared for the child. Some seem directed at you. In general, penalties that affect your child's personal time (like detention) are geared for him. Penalties affecting grades (at least in the early years) are speaking to you. Underlying both types of penalties is an implicit notion that your child can do the work, and that you can make him do it.

I believe this assumption is wrong. I call this the *Myth of Motivation,* and I assert that the child is homework trapped, because he has some difficulty learning the material. By missing this point and addressing motivation, the child is stuck in an irresolvable bind, asked to do something he really can't do. In response, he looks for ways to cope, and the strategies he finds are often deemed as *bad behavior.*

To explain my premise, I'll start by talking about why people (children or adults) do the things they do. Simply stated, we do the things we want to do. We do things we can do. Let me draw a picture from my personal experience.

I have a good friend who sings with a prestigious amateur choir. I play tennis each week with a group of comparably skilled tennis players. We engage in these different activities because we want to and because we can.

Imagine what would happen if there were compulsory choir laws, and I was forced to join my friend's choir group? As a good citizen, I would likely comply and come to practice. It would not take long before my lack of skill began to show. I might try to blend in and work hard at first. As I fell behind, I would look for ways to escape the situation. I might miss practice or come late to the concert. I might get sick in the middle of rehearsals. I might just stand and mouth the words without making sounds. I might make jokes and act like a clown. If confronted to explain my behavior, I might just say, "I dunno." Whatever I chose to do, keep in mind that the one option I don't have is to sing. I simply lack the skill to sing at a level that would keep me from standing out in my friend's group (just as he would slow down the pace if he joined my tennis group).

Of course, there are no compulsory choir or tennis laws, and you may be asking, "Aren't there things we have to do?" Absolutely. Consider taxes. Even though we don't want to, my friend and I pay our income tax. How does that happen? Is it because we fear the consequences and don't want to go to jail?

Certainly, that plays a part in the decisions we make, but there is something more. We pay our taxes because we *can*. Between payroll withholding, computer tax programs, and public accountants, we have a range of options for successfully paying our taxes, whether or not we understand how to do it or have the self-discipline to put our money away.

How Do You Know If It's Interests or Skills?

Even with this model, it is likely that many teachers will still want to know, before changing their approach, if it is a learning problem. How do you know if the issue is interests or skills? You probably don't, and you probably can't know. Most likely, it's a little of both. But here's the key: *It doesn't matter.* Even if the problem were *motivational,* the solution is still *educational*.

You've already acted as if motivation were the problem. If it hasn't worked, it's time to move on.

There's a cardinal rule in psychology: Good consequences are ones that end. You know when a penalty works, because you don't have to use it anymore. Points off and zeros are great for some children. Get them once, and they don't happen again.

These children feel ashamed, fear disapproval, and want to do well. They have experienced good grades most of the time. Since penalties work for them, this seems to confirm the motivational model. Yet, they don't work for every child. If consequences were effective, we would know this for one basic reason: They stopped! The sign of a good penalty is that it is not needed again.

If penalties that don't work continue to be used, they have an opposite effect from what was intended, and this is what happens with the homework-trapped child. After all, the child keeps failing. He gets zeros and points off over and over again. People assume that the child is flawed. While this is partly true (in reference to some not-yet-understood learning problem), it is also true that the system is flawed, at least for the child. The fact that the child continues to miss recess, takes afterschool detentions, and listens daily to critical lectures is a strong sign that the system is not working, and its underlying notion (poor motivation) must be wrong. Yet, despite this evidence, people continue to believe that he would do so much better, if he just tried.

There are reasons why this notion persists. First, it seems fair. After all, the other children face the same conditions. Why not the homework-trapped child? Second, the child sometimes does the work. If he did it once, why can't he do it again? Third, he does work at school. Why can't he do it at home? Fourth, it's policy. Change the standards, and it might interfere with what the other children do.

I understand that teachers will be reluctant to make some of the changes that I recommend. Yet, whatever their hesitation, your child may need a different approach. *Fairness* is hardly relevant to you when your child keeps falling down. The fact that he sometimes does the work does not mean he can always do the work. There may be differences in subjects, types of assignments, overall volume, and which teacher gives the work.

The fact that he works at school does not mean he can work at home. Home and school are different settings. They have different cultures, norms, standards, and designs. They each operate at different times of day. There is no trained teacher present in your home to intervene when the child is stuck.

I suspect that, in the end, policy is the reason why the standard is not changed. Yet, there is a foundation to give allowances for children who cannot conform to the norm. Under federal law, children with disabilities are entitled to accommodations through an individualized educational plan. Children with health problems who fall short of this classification can also have accommodations under a 504 plan. The problem for homework-trapped children is that their difficulties are not recognized for the learning problems they are, so accommodations do not kick in until academics suffer and the behavior gets worse. The accommodations then focus on behavioral, not learning, problems, and they inevitably serve to make things worse. The homework relief that the child eventually receives is when he gets excluded from the regular class or school. This leaves classroom policy undisturbed by homework accommodations, while failing to support an inclusion solution.

But I'm Sure He Can Do It!

Not convinced. Take another tack. Consider this idea: Interests beget skills, and skills beget interests. Remember, we're looking for solutions, not simply harping on problems.

I told you before that I am a tennis player. Now, I'll tell you why. When I was little, I wanted to play baseball like most other boys. No one—my teachers, my parents, my friends—questioned the strength of my interest. I did not start out wanting to play tennis.

Unfortunately, the realities were clear. I couldn't throw the ball straight, I ran very slowly, and I rarely caught the ball. I got two mandatory innings in right field while my coach and teammates prayed the ball would not come my way. It did not take long for me to stop signing up for Little League.

At twelve years of age, my *non-athletic* friends and I found some old tennis racquets and headed for the court. Lo and behold, I proved to be the one most capable of hitting a tennis ball over the net. Since tennis was not yet a popular sport, I could rise quickly to the top of the group without competing with the *athletic boys.* By high school, my skills had improved to the point that I was highly competitive with other youth when it came time to try out for the school tennis team. My skill (rewarded in relation to a selected subgroup) created an interest. With interest, I went on to develop considerable skill.

It's a fact of human nature that we move toward activities where we do well, and we become better at the things we like to do. Although many contend that homework compliance is essential for learning good work habits, I argue that it's the *perception* of school success that sows the seeds for later high school and college success. There are many children who excel in later years, while they did little *homework* when they were young. They did their assignments, just not at home. They found it easy and had ample time after school for personal pursuits. Still, they received accolades for their diligence, even though they did not try hard, and academics never interfered with play. By the time these children faced a need to buckle down, they did what they needed to pass the course. They had not acquired study habits. They acquired self-confidence, which helped them get ahead.

If your child is to become homework successful, he needs to believe that he is doing well. Things will not change if he continues to receive daily consequences for work not done, based on the assumption that it's a motivational lag. It does not matter if there is some truth to the fact that he does not want to do the work. Skills beget interests. Interests beget skills. You need to start by insuring that he can do the work. Even more, you need to insure that *he* believes he can do it.

3. BEHAVIORAL FACTORS

Homework takes place at home. Overseeing your child's homework is a job that belongs to you as a parent. You may have no training in how to parent. You may parent differently than your neighbors do. You may not be fully effective as a parent. You may be a better parent for one of your children than another. If you tell your child that he has to rake the yard, you can praise him for his yard-raking, even if he did less than you thought he should have done. Maybe, he'll do better next time. You don't have that option with homework, since you do not control the assignment or the grade.

There are several factors that sustain behavior. Here, I will talk about two concepts from behavioral learning theory—classical and operant conditioning—and how they help us understand your child's problems with homework.

Classical Conditioning

Ivan Pavlov, a Russian psychologist, described classical conditioning. In his famous study (1927), Pavlov taught a dog to salivate to the sound of a bell. He rang a bell before showing the hungry dog food. At first, the dog salivated at the sight of food. Before long, it salivated at the sound of the bell. The bell became associated with food and caused his body to react, as if he were about to get fed.

Say you lived on a farm and were working in the field. It's close to dinnertime, but you have not thought about food. The dinner bell rings. Suddenly, you are famished.

Words elicit feelings based on what they mean. If we served you lemon meringue pie, you might break into a smile, brighten up, and anticipate a tasty treat, or you might shudder because you don't like its taste.

Now, stop reading and think of what you are experiencing. Are you tasting and smelling lemons? Does it feel good? Are you shuddering at the thought? This book is not published on lemon-scented paper. If you had a reaction, it is coming from the words, not from a pie.

Let's try another word:

Sex

How did you react? Feel good? Embarrassed? What are your associations?

Try another:

Vomit

What now?

For each of these words, you have some mental image, possibly pleasant, possibly revolting, depending on the experiences you have had in the past.

Years ago, I visited a highly rated vegetarian restaurant known for its mushroom barley soup. I tried it and became violently ill that evening. There was something wrong with my bowl of soup. I had food poisoning. For years I could not hear the words, *mushroom barley*, without feeling sick (I feel a bit queasy writing these words now).

Let's try another word:

Homework

What does this word make you feel? What does the word do to a star student, one who has never faced homework difficulties? How about your child?

I call "homework" the H-word. How often do you use it every day? If you are like most parents embroiled in homework battles, you feel constant pressure to get your child going. You think about homework nearly all the time and remind your child whenever you can. The battles are painful, and the word, homework, has become associated with that pain. It creates panic in you and anger in your child the moment the H-word is said.

Operant Learning

B.F Skinner was also a psychologist, and he developed a model called operant conditioning. Whereas Pavlov dealt with gut, emotional reactions (the technical term is autonomic), Skinner looked at patterns of learned behavior (1938). He showed that if an action is rewarded, it is more likely to reoccur. If an action is punished, it's less likely to happen again. The current grading system rests on this idea. Do the work, and you earn a reward. Don't do the work, and you suffer a penalty. Through these consequences, it's hoped that the child will develop good habits. This notion is well grounded in behavioral learning theory, and, in many cases, it works. For your child, it may not. Let's look further into this theory, which is foundational to current educational practice, so we can understand what may be happening with your child.

There have been many experiments involving laboratory animals (usually white rats) using what is called a "Skinner box." The box is a cage with a lever on one side. The lever is designed to offer different outcomes when it is pushed. To give a positive reward, it delivers a pellet of food to the animal. For the negative consequence, it gives a small electric shock. By varying the frequency and conditions under which these consequences are given, psychologists study how simple learning occurs. Predictably, the animal receiving food will continue to push the food-bearing lever. The animal that gets a shock will not touch the lever again.

Psychologists have learned that it is easier to retrain the animal that has been taught through reward than the one that has been taught through punishment. If scientists stop offering food, the animal will soon stop pressing that lever. If scientists stop giving shocks, the animal *will not* start pushing the lever again. In a similar vein, the student who has had school success and learned through rewards should prove more flexible down the line. The student who has failed and has often been punished will prove more rigid and unable to learn new things.

To get that animal to start pushing the formerly shock-giving lever, scientists need to *shape* lever-pushing behavior. Shaping essentially means offering reward for partial success. You must reward the animal as it ventures close, even if it has not yet touched the lever. Similarly, to get the student to undo homework problems, it's important to increase the rewards for small increments of success.

In school, a fixed grading system usually administers punishments and rewards. For the group, the system may work. For the individual, it may not. Conceptually, the system can be thought of as a type of Skinner box, with levers dispensing punishments and rewards. It is not surprising that educators use this model. After all, they are concerned about behavior, and they bank on the theories discussed here. The problem is not the system itself, but how the system adjusts (or fails to) for the child who is not operating as hoped for, according to the paradigm.

There's another fact about experiments in operant conditioning that may seem trivial but is quite important. It's the box itself. I don't know of any experimental psychologists conducting studies using a lever without a cage. This is for a good reason: There would be too much risk of the animal running around the room and leaving the lab. If the animal touched the lever once, it is possible that the animal might come back if it was a food-bearing lever, and there was no other good source of food in the room. For the animal that touched the shock-delivering lever, unlearning would prove virtually impossible, since the animal would not venture close enough to the lever to shape the response. Similarly, the homework-trapped child has usually developed such effective ways to avoid doing homework that is if very difficult to get that child to even start the work.

Applying Learning Principles

Putting this altogether, there are two learning principles that are relevant to the acquisition of homework-doing habits. Ideally, children develop positive associations to the concept of education and develop productive study habits that are reinforced by success. In contrast, the homework-trapped child has developed negative associations to the H-word itself and does not get rewards but is mired in penalties.

To correct this, there are several steps that can be taken. Some, parents can do on their own. Some require that the school be on board. In general, the goals are the following:

Decondition the child's negative feelings about homework.

Help him give up his avoidant strategies.

Deconditioning Negative Feelings

Right now, you and your child may get upset every time the topic of homework comes up. He may have an immediate and negative reaction to any reference you make about his homework. Most likely, you feel the same way. Talk about homework, and you may be in a high-tension zone. You need to alter those associations, which means both you and he have to create different feelings when you use the H-word. You can do this by reducing the frequency with which you mention homework and altering the emotions with which you say it.

This won't be easy. After all, you may be frustrated to the hilt with your child's behavior. You may feel pressured by the school and possibly embarrassed too. Homework may constantly be on your mind. You can't easily will yourself to feel a different way. Still, the patterns have been set in place, and the word represents pain. Just as Pavlov's dog salivated to the bell, you and your child may cringe at the word.

Each time you restrain yourself from using the H-word, you have taken a step toward deconditioning its effect. Each time you use it, but say it without emotion, you have taken a further step.

To restrain its use, limit yourself to mentioning homework no more than twice a day—once at the start, and once when homework ends. Use other terminology for anything you say in between.

You can reduce the tension further by saying fewer words and not asking for a response. Say, "Homework time," instead of asking, "Have you started your homework yet?" Say, "Let me see what you did," instead of asking, "Did you get your homework done?" Smile when you talk, pat him on the back, keep the tone light, resist the temptation to give him a lecture, employ humor, and reduce the panic that this is a moral or pressing problem. Avoid verbal scripts in which you find yourself saying what did not work the day before. Say things once. Bypass conflict as much as you can.

Operant Learning

The homework-trapped child has developed a wide range of avoidant behaviors. Although they are considered "bad behaviors,"—lying, procrastinating, arguing, misplacing, and forgetting—they are actually methods he uses to cope. These behaviors are strongly reinforced since they shield the child from a painful experience. For the laboratory animal, it's a simple matter of staying away from the shock-bearing lever. For human beings, the pain is far more complex. Keep in mind that the child is being asked to do something he cannot do.

Unlearning avoidant behaviors requires shaping, and this means access to reward for partial success. The child needs support and praise for what he can do, not criticism and punishment for what he can't do.

You need to redefine the goal from full success now to full success later on. You need to give your child full rewards for progressively increasing examples of partial success. At some point, you may have to confront a difference in philosophy between you and the school, since the school takes points off for the work that isn't done. Later in this book, we'll address ways for you to deal with the school. Right now, you need to stay focused on what is true, which is that your child may not succeed without shaping better behavior.

There are some techniques that you can use. First, set time limits. If your child knows that there is a time after which he can leave, he'll have less need to avoid work. He does not have to lie about getting the work done if *getting it all done* is not required to bring his homework time to an end.

The second technique is reward. Start by excluding all criticism for the work he has not done. Comment on the fact that he did 10 percent, 20 percent, or 50 percent of the assignments that he had. If he does nothing at all, stay calm, praise him for staying in his room without distractions, and suggest he'll do better tomorrow.

Third, you can reframe the notion of "criticism" by directing it to the work, not to him as a person. If you deem the problem to be his character, you'll be dealing with his character. If you agree that it's the work (he probably has said that the assignment is too hard), you'll be dealing with the work.

Fourth, create a *criticism standard.* For example, limit yourself to one negative comment a night. Another approach is to give four comments or gestures of support for every critical comment you make. Express your criticisms with emotional neutrality or use humor when you deliver a negative statement. Keep in mind that the existing system provides strong reinforcement for your child to avoid work. You want to alter those terms so he can now comply.

4. MODELING and MATURATION

"If he doesn't do it now, he'll be in trouble later on," your child's teacher says as you meet to discuss his homework problem. "It only gets harder in the later years. By high school, he won't know what to do."

Behind this statement, there is the common-sense notion that education is progressive, and that the things children learn in the earlier grades prepare them for harder work later on. Develop homework skills and good study habits now, and you'll be ready for high school and college. If a few minutes of homework at night set the stage for later success, I'd be all for that.

Unfortunately, the point in your home may be moot. You might be the parent of a homework-trapped child, and, if so, you will not see these desirable effects. You could have a hard time pointing to the evidence, in your home, that homework was having any value at all. Yet, you're still told that *if he doesn't do it now, he'll be in trouble later on.* Let's examine that notion and consider if it's true. Even if homework compliance can prepare children for future success, is it the *only way?* Are we certain that the homework-trapped child, if freed from the pressure he's under right now, has no other chance later on? In answering this question, we'll consider modeling and maturation.

Modeling and maturation are two forces that affect human behavior. They take place in a context in which the individual feels connected to his environment and supported by others. To the degree that the homework experience separates the child from others and keeps him feeling under pressure and criticized, it actually thwarts rather than enhances these components of learning.

Social Modeling

Social modeling is a concept developed by Albert Bandura. He claimed that humans acquire habits by imitating the behaviors of others, without requiring punishment or reward (1977). We watch people act, and we act the way they do. When young, parents are our most notable models. As we get older, teachers, public figures, and peers also serve as role models. Good homework behaviors can be acquired, if the child has models that support this.

Consider our prior farm example. The farmhand felt hungry at the sound of the dinner bell. He makes his way back to the farmhouse. What happens there? Does he go to the table and start digging in? Does he scoop up the food with his hands? If he gets there first, does he eat before the others arrive? Most likely, there is a sequence of behaviors that takes place before the farmhand eats. He may take a place at the table and wait. He may bow his head when someone says a prayer. He may pass the bowl and wait until everyone is served. Most likely, he uses utensils instead of his hands.

The farmhand may have learned these behaviors where he grew up. But even if he was raised in a home where people dug in without saying grace, ate with their hands, and spit on the floor, he is likely to watch the others and comply with the house norms. No one had to teach him. He did what he saw.

To model desired behaviors, one has to have access to good models. Further, positive feelings between the person and the model facilitate modeling. The uncouth farmhand learns good manners, because he eats with the farm family and wants a place in the group. The homework-trapped child may develop good homework habits later on, when he's placed in an environment with others who do their work. Many homework-trapped children who manage to get to college actually do better there, despite the greater demands.

Consider this difference between high school and college (for the person who lives on campus). A typical high school student spends about thirty hours a week in class and five to fifteen hours working by himself at home. A typical college student spends twelve to sixteen hours a week in class and twenty-four to thirty hours doing work in his dorm. The high school student sees his friends in class and his parents at home. The college student may not have friends in his classes, but generally has them where he lives in the dorm. The college student does not come "home" to parents telling him what to do, but to other students who may be studying for their tests. The forces of modeling increase the chance that your high school unsuccessful child will now do his work in college.

Parents are the first and foremost models. Your child watches everything you do. Your personal habits have a large effect on him. Consider what you do when you are at home.

Do you read a book? Do you watch TV shows with educational value? Do you engage in thoughtful and lively debate? Do you perform household chores with a smile on your face? Or do you squander your time? Are you yelling at your spouse and frequently getting drunk? Are you sleeping on the couch or playing video games? Whatever you do, keep in mind that you are being watched.

Obviously, parents are different; families are different. I don't judge the things you do and fully respect your right to the choices you make for your life. But homework has a way of stripping you of that choice. You feel beholden to an external authority (the teachers and the school) to make decisions about what happens in your house. Your behavior may change, as you feel panicked to make sure that the work gets done.

If you yell at your child, you are modeling yelling behavior. If you make idle threats, you are modeling how to be an ineffective adult. If you are doing the work for your child out of fear that he will otherwise fail, you are modeling cheating. Further, you have less time to do the things you otherwise would do. You may feel too tired to sit down and read that book. You may be so stressed out that you unwind with a mindless TV show. Further, you may be forcing your son to sit at a desk in his room and stare at his books. This deprives him of time he could be spending with you and watching you.

Teachers are models, too. They are society's symbols for education. They have gone to college and are educated themselves.

They interact with your child in the task of learning. If your child's teacher exudes joy in learning, you child is likely to follow her lead. If the teacher is disgruntled, your child is more likely to dislike school. And if your child's teacher loves her work and likes your child, but keeps getting angry at him throughout the school day, he will feel her disapproval and start to pull away. Poor grades and ongoing criticism taint the relationship and spoil the model. By the end of the year, your child may no longer see that teacher as a person to emulate.

Peers are models. Undoubtedly, your child mimics the habits and mannerisms of his good friends and of those children who seem to do well. The models your child picks will often depend on the type of success he seeks. If he wants to be an A student, he'll seek out peers who are A students. If he wants to be *cool*, he'll look for those who have had social success. If his friends are children who start to smoke, he's more likely to start smoking. If they don't, that behavior is less likely to occur. If your child spends time with children who do well in school, he's more likely to do well himself. If his friends don't care and don't do their work, his interest is likely to wane, too.

Let's consider how your child's homework experience affects the modeling process for him at different grades. In elementary school, your child will be placed in a class with other children from the neighborhood. In general, there will be expected norms of behavior, which include doing one's homework every day. If your child chronically fails to do his work, he will feel shame and believe the *good student* role is out of his reach. This will propel him to look for a different role, often that of *class dummy* or *class clown*. He may get comfortable with the status of the one who never does his work. In fact, he may reach a point where it becomes embarrassing for him to break from that role. Many homework-trapped children don't hand in their work even when it has been done. They don't want the attention they get for veering from their role.

By middle school, the task becomes considerably more complex, with the teacher feeling pressured to reach higher standards. With more teachers assigning work, the homework-trapped child flounders even more. Remedial placement may follow, and this moves the child farther away from peers who value work.

In high school, there is an added factor, which is athletic participation. Eligibility requirements, designed so that sports would support school, often work in reverse for the homework-trapped child. These children don't have the skill to keep up with their work. They lose their sports and, with that, their desire to ever get back on track. Since most community-based sports leagues end with the eighth grade, the child has no place to play except on the high school team. This pushes the child farther toward peer groups that model negative behaviors.

Maturation

Maturation is another important factor when considering how we learn. There are skills that we are taught, and others we develop when we become old enough. Although learning builds up from year to year, there are parts of that process that we simply grow into.

For a child to be successful at any grade level, he must have the maturity to handle what is entailed. There is a reason why six-year-old children go to first grade and seven-year-old children are assigned to second grade. Efforts to push bright children ahead by having them skip grades rarely work.

Although school is designed with child development in mind, it is also designed to function at its task, which is teaching children. It's important to have annually graded classes from one to twelve, so that teachers can plan curricula appropriate for each class. There needs to be some basis to put enough children in the same room, despite the differences they may individually display.

Even so, we know that there are marked variations in emotional development between children in single grades. Girls are more mature than boys. Children born in October are much older than their classmates born the following September.[1] Children with serious illnesses may not mature at the expected rate. Even if they get better, their earlier health experiences may thwart how quickly they grow up. Children born prematurely are less mature than those with the same birthday who were born full term. A child born in September with a December due date will be developmentally far behind the others in his class.

When differences in development are truly severe, the child study team may come in. For the child who has an *under-the-radar* learning or developmental problem (as many homework-trapped children do), it does not make sense to classify that child. Yet, minor problems the child has during the day get magnified dramatically with the homework task. Whereas that child may

---

1   In New Jersey where the author resides, the cutoff date for school registration is October 1.

struggle to sit still during class, it's beyond his capacity to sit still later on.

Eventually, your child grows up and becomes an adult. Hopefully, he will have a lot of skills. You want him to learn. But even if he has not learned as well as you would have liked, he'll be better prepared to handle adulthood if he feels good about himself. Obviously, some things are vital. You do not want your child passing through the first years of school without learning how to read. You want your child to acquire a foundation of basic math and language skills. But you also want your child to be prepared to learn later on, even if things don't fit together now.

So back to the claim of *"If he doesn't do it now, he'll be in trouble later on."* Are we sure this is true? If your child has learned to hate school, this may be true. But keep in mind that although homework is part of the formula for learning, learning can still take place, even if the homework has not been done. After all, the majority of your child's educational time takes place in school, not in your home. If pressure to do homework influences your child's experience too much, his distaste for school will over-shadow the positive effects maturation provides.

5. the SYSTEMS EFFECT

"Let's bring this meeting to order," your child's principal says, as you, his guidance counselor, the school nurse, and two teachers sit around a table, trying to figure out what to do, now that your son has gotten into a fight. This is the first time the principal has gotten involved. You've had many prior meetings with your child's teachers over homework noncompliance, his coming late to class, his clowning around, and other minor behavioral infractions. Nothing you've tried seems to have worked. Now, the problems are getting a lot worse.

You know your son is having a hard time, and you try to explain what you think is going on. All eyes turn to the principal, seeming to look for direction from him. You're always told you're part of the team. Somehow, you feel very much alone.

Understanding Systems

Schools are highly complex systems. They have their organizational hierarchies, with lines of command traveling down from
the school superintendent (the CEO) to the classroom teacher.
There are assistant superintendents and principals (middle man-
agers) in between, other educational professionals (e.g., the members of the child study team), with a cast of non-educators (such
as the building and administrative support staff) as well. These
individuals relate to each other through lines of authority, which
are usually described on an organizational chart. They may have
clear or muddied lines of authority. They have formal and informal means of communication. When you talk with your child's
teacher, you are interacting with a person who also serves as the
face of this complex organization. How much authority and control that teacher has, and what goes into the decisions he or she
makes, may depend heavily on the dynamics of that system. For
sure, that individual has ongoing, working relationships with
other people that extend far beyond concerns for your child.

• SYSTEMS CHART I •

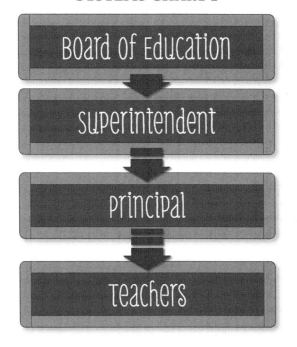

Your family is a system, too. You have a range of customs, habits, hierarchies, and structures. Your family may have one or two heads of the home. There may be extended family with considerable influence on how your family works. You may have lots of space where your child can do his work, or much smaller quarters, where several siblings must share common space. Undoubtedly, you have a home, which reflects your experiences, beliefs, personality, and means.

For the most part, school is school, and home is home. These systems operate independently of each other, with your child accountable to different authorities at different times of the day. Homework is an anomaly that traverses these natural lines. It is an activity that has been defined at school to take place in your home. It is offered as policy, not as a suggestion, with the school having the power to punish if it does not get done. Although homework is not the only demand on your child's time that comes from outside your home, it is the most tenacious. You may sign your child up to study piano, but if he does not practice, the choices are yours. You may penalize him, stop the lessons, find another teacher, or maintain the status quo, even though he is not learning very well. The choice is yours, and the impact of his behavior, if he is piano-practice-noncompliant, on his life is slight. He is not in a piano trap, but he may be in a homework trap. For homework, the expectation continues regardless of what you do, and the consequences for the future may prove quite severe.

For parents of children without homework problems, this point is moot. Even if they disagree with how much work the teachers are sending home, they keep their thoughts private and simply expect their children to comply. For you, this issue may loom large. Homework might have become a major event in your home, not just something your child handles by himself. To understand what is happening, it is helpful to consider how these systems (home and school) collide. First, we'll consider you're child's relationship with his school. Then, we'll consider what may have happened to you, as you and the school work together to solve your child's problem.

Your Child and the School

Your child goes to school five days a week, nine months of the year, for thirteen years, from kindergarten to the twelfth grade. He is expected to "work." He receives periodic performance reviews, with his advancement depending on what he does. From the school's point of view, your child is a client. From a different perspective, your child's role is much more that of an employee than a consumer. Although he does not receive a paycheck, he fits well conceptually on the school's organizational chart, where he is placed at the bottom.

• SYSTEMS CHART II •

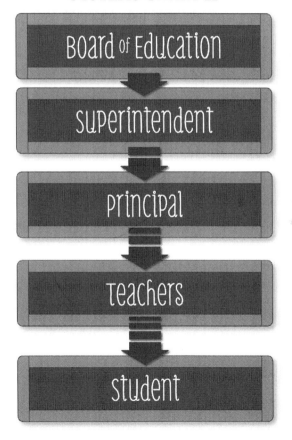

Board of Education

↓

Superintendent

↓

Principal

↓

Teachers

↓

Student

When your child starts school, he reports to one teacher. By upper elementary school, there are often two teachers who work as a team. By middle school, there may be four or five teachers organized in teams. By high school, his teachers are more allied with their subject departments than they are with each other. With each progressive move through the system, the demands on your child get more complex.

Through organizational theory, we know that employees function best when lines of authority are simple and clear. Where there must be conditions of dual reportability, it's important to make sure that the demands do not compete with each other. If your child were truly a *customer* of the school, once he reached middle school he would move from class to class, consuming the products that were offered there. Using the *student as employee* model, organizational theory predicts (since your child reports to several different bosses with equal amounts of authority) that this is a difficult way to work. For sure, good teamwork among teachers mitigates this effect. Of course, the prospects for such teamwork decrease dramatically as the child moves through the upper grades.

Although this demand is complex, the structure of the day lessens its effects. After all, students have a schedule that tells them where to go at any time of the day. Unfortunately, that structure breaks down at night. Then, assignments converge into a common unit of time, calling on the child to balance competing demands. Although the transition is intrinsically difficult, the child who has been successful in the earlier years enters upper grades able to rise to the task. The child whose experience was laden with failure and criticism lacks the foundation to take this leap. These children do what employees typically do when handling competing demands from multiple bosses. They pick and choose what they will do. For example, they may do everything for one teacher and nothing for another.

Many homework-trapped children start each year fully committed to turning things around. Yet, they don't have the skills to manage the workload. So they let their classes go, one at a time. Rather than garnering recognition for the effort they tried to put out, they get hit with low grades and criticism for what they did not do. In the end, they feel overwhelmed and do nothing at all.

Children who are chronically homework-trapped need a single leader to tell them what to do. They cannot manage multiple demands from several different teachers on their own. Unfortunately, that need sometimes gets met through the *back door,* as the child moves from a homework problem to a behavioral problem and on to special-education placement outside the regular classroom. For the child who is intellectually capable but homework-trapped, this can be ego-deflating and a path toward eventually dropping out of school. I recommend a simple accommodation of a lead/study-skills teacher for homework-trapped children in the upper grades.

This lead teacher would do the following:

1. Monitor a small, structured study hall for the child.
2. Teach study skills on an individualized basis.
3. Serve as the primary contact for the parent.
4. Prioritize assignments among different teachers.
5. Maintain authority to waive requirements to comply with the time-based principle.

This solution may prove complicated for teachers. After all, it requires that they make decisions among themselves about which assignments stay, and which ones go. For the homework-trapped child, it plays a crucial role in helping him manage the homework assignments that he has not, so far, been able to do. It reconfigures his relationships with the teachers. He goes from having multiple bosses to now reporting to a single, key authority. Obviously, the child would still be fully accountable to the individual teacher whose class he was in at any given time.

You and the School

Now let's return to your role on the school's organizational chart. I have already hinted that you should be careful about how you become *part of the team.* Here, we'll see what team membership can do to the relationship you have with your child.

Without homework problems, the natural hierarchies look like the following:

School System

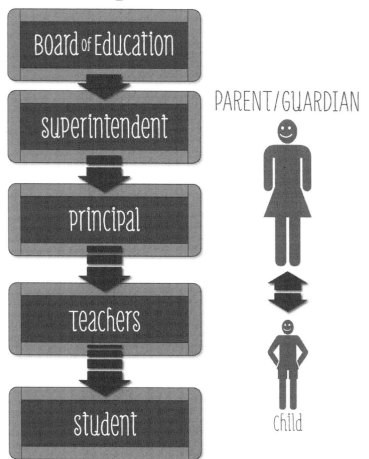

Here, we see two distinct organizations, which are the family and the school. The child belongs to each system. The school is in charge during school hours, and the parents accept the assignments that come home. The systems operate cooperatively but separately, with neither being particularly in charge of the other.

Now let's see what can happen if you partner with the school, as if you're a member of the team. By thinking of your child *as-if* he were an employee of the school and of you *as-if* you were on the school's organizational chart, we see dynamics in place that make homework noncompliance more likely to go on. You and the school may try to be a team, yet you are not. You lack the fundamental components necessary for good teamwork. You are meeting about your child alone. You are outside discussions involving other students. You have no informal lines of communication with your team members. You never sit down just to take a break together.

This breeds distrust on both sides of the fence. It is just as understandable for the school to perceive you as creating problems as it is for you to perceive the school that way. It's not that either party means ill. It's that you have forsaken a fundamental of good cooperative work, which is to recognize the true nature of your relationship. You are not a member of the school's team (even if your child has an IEP, and you are defined that way by federal law). You are leaders of separate groups coming together over a shared concern. And you cannot sustain that role as long as final authority over what happens in your home remains in the hands of someone other than you.

With homework, the parent lacks authority to define the task. Consequently, the parent is left with an enforcement role. This necessarily places the parent in a de facto position with the school that looks like the following:

School System

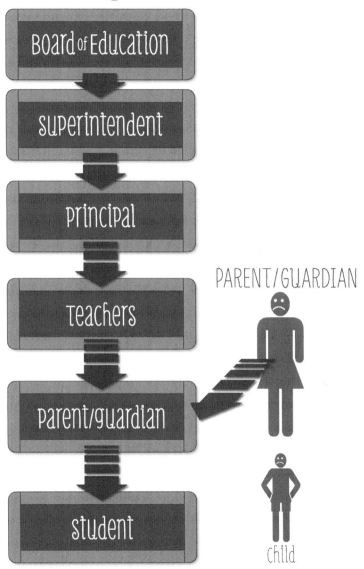

From an organizational perspective, there is no way for the parent to succeed. The loss of authority with the child is much too great for the family to function well. Further, the role you take as the enforcer of school rules actually compromises your standing on other issues that take place in the home.

To be an effective parent for a homework-trapped child, you must remain head of the home. To create a better parent-school relationship, two components must be in place. First, the parent needs to have the ultimate authority over what happens in the home. Second, the parent needs a single representative from the school with whom to hold discussions and work out the homework problem. Again, my model of a lead/study-skills teacher proves vital for your child's success in the upper grades.

The Risks Involved

There are well-meaning teachers and parents meeting every day without ever stepping back to consider the structures in which they work. They focus on the problem, not the process, and don't understand why tensions grow large while the child does not change. Both are frustrated, and it is natural to see fault on the other side. Yet, it's the unquestioned structure of the team model that is fanning the flames. On one side of the table, there are people with training. On the other side, there are untrained parents. As the problem grows large, pressure mounts for parents to do what the professionals say.

You may be scratching your head and wondering why this is a problem. After all, isn't this what professionals are paid to do? To teach children and give parents advice on how to help out?

This is true to the extent that the advice given is based on the expertise these professionals have. As it is, teachers are trained to teach, not in the art of giving out homework. There are no textbooks or courses in schools of education on the theory and practice of homework and its problems. Homework is a policy, not a teaching technique, and it is not well supported by research (see Cooper, 2001, for review of the research).

It also happens that school psychologists are not trained in resolving homework problems. They are well trained in other issues vital to your child's well being and success, but not in this particular problem. If you look at the lessons from Chapter 2 through Chapter 5, you will realize that I have just given you a mini-course in the theories of psychology. I've covered such topics as motivation, classical conditioning, operant learning, social modeling, maturation, and organizational theory. Although school psychologists are familiar with these concepts, they have not been taught to apply them to the particular problems of homework noncompliance.

One final note from developmental psychology: In the end, children need parents who are in charge. Parents are flawed, and children need to deal with their own parents' mistakes. Through the years they are in school, children go through many different feelings toward their parents, and this is part of a process through which they eventually find themselves. They idealize their parents while in the lower grades. They may fault their parents mercilessly when they are teens. Regardless of what stage they are in, they need to know that their parents are there. It assaults their sense of safety and security to see their parents floundering around, trying to enforce rules which they do not believe in.

Children need direction from their parents. They also need to get an education. Although homework has its place in learning, it becomes counterproductive when it dominates the process. This notion does not apply to other aspects of education, since they take place in someone else's house (the school). In the end, homework-trapped children lose out on two things they need: powerful parents and a quality education.

6. the LEARNING PROBLEM

E arlier in this book, I suggested that there are *under-the-radar* learning problems at the root of your child's homework struggle. Let's consider what those problems are, and what you can do about them.

There are two primary sources of chronic homework deficiencies, and they are problems with working memory and processing speed. These issues should be well known to the school, since they constitute two of the four major factors of what is commonly thought of as intelligence. The other two areas are verbal comprehension and perceptual reasoning.

When psychologists assess a child's IQ, one of the two instruments they most commonly use is the Wechsler Intelligence Scale for Children—Fourth Edition (2003). This test generates intelligence quotients in each of these four areas (verbal comprehension, perceptual reasoning, working memory, and processing speed), and then combines those results into a full-scale IQ. If the school's child study team has evaluated your child, it is likely that he has been given this test. Sadly, schools often overlook the implications this important test (and the concepts behind it) has regarding the child's ability to complete his homework. In general, verbal comprehension and perceptual reasoning coincide with what we think of when we look at a child and form an impression of how bright that child may be. In contrast, working memory and processing speed have bearing on the child's ability to act on those potentials and do successful work. Children with strengths in verbal comprehension and perceptual reasoning, but who have weaknesses in working memory and/or processing speed, are often misperceived with statements such as, "You're so bright, and you could make As if you only tried." In fact, these children can learn at the A level, but they'll still have difficulty performing at that grade level. They also have considerably more difficulty completing their homework than they do completing work they are given in school. Since teachers see the child at school, but not at home, they may have trouble comprehending just how difficult it is for the child to work at home.

Consider this question: Is the purpose of school to learn or to perform? If it is to learn, we get farther by rewarding the child for what he has learned, rather than overly focusing on his difficulty performing. If the purpose is just to perform, then we risk compromising his education in the service of performance at a particular task, creating a self-fulfilling prophesy of a child who fails to do well.

Working Memory

We'll start with working memory, and consider what that is. Simply stated, working memory refers to our capacity to hold onto information while thinking about other things. Try the following problem: John has fifteen marbles. He gives three of his friends four marbles each. How many marbles does he have left? This is not a difficult problem, if you write it down. It becomes more difficult when presented in verbal form. The child may know that $3X4=12$ and that $15-12=3$, but he'll give the wrong answer if he forgets the number fifteen, while calculating $3X4$. It's working memory that allows that child to hold onto that number, while tackling the first part of the problem.

Much of what your child learns in school and is told to do is presented in verbal form. Do you recall *Peanuts*, the cartoon, and the character Linus? One recurring bit from this cartoon involved Linus sitting in class, listening to his teacher, who said, "Mwa, mwa, mwa." For the child with poor working memory, that's exactly how the teacher sounds much of the time.

In today's society, we are well oriented to the notion of problems with attention. The diagnosis of ADHD has exploded in recent years. Working memory is a closely allied concept to that of attention. The child who cannot absorb and hold onto much verbally presented material hears, "Mwa, mwa, mwa," while looking as if he is not paying attention. Certainly, interventions that heighten the child's attention will help that child hold onto and remember more of what that teacher says. But keep in mind, even though the child may appear more focused, the inherent and underlying problem of poor working memory still persists. I should note that when psychologists measure a child's working memory (the WISC-IV has three working-memory subtests: Digit Span, Letter-Number Sequencing, and Arithmetic), it is done through one-on-one administration in a controlled environment. The psychologist takes care to recruit the child's attention, yet that child may still have difficulty completing those tasks. Imagine the difficulties that child has paying attention in class, and then trying to remember what he needs to do when he gets home.

Processing Speed

The other problem involves processing speed. The WISC-IV has three subtests—Coding, Symbol Search, and Cancellation—that measure processing speed. All three are timed tests and highly sensitive to the child's capacity to work quickly. Coding is unique among the tests, in that it requires the child to reproduce specific symbols (in contrast to the others, in which the child simply crosses out his answer). The results of coding are particularly germane to the issue of homework performance, in that the task is most closely allied to handwriting skills.

In the early elementary school grades, when children begin to form ideas about how smart they are, speed plays a critical role. Think about your experiences as an elementary school child. Do you remember taking tests and completing other assignments, and looking up to see who else was done? Was everyone still working after you finished? Did that make you feel you were bright? Or was the teacher waiting, impatiently, for you, the last one, to complete your work? Children are sensitive to these differences in pace, and they incorporate this into the views they have of themselves. Children with slow handwriting, poor handwriting, or handwriting fatigue (i.e., their hand gets tired and hurts) are at a disadvantage when it comes to school performance. It's not surprising that most homework problems (and the reason for my politically incorrect use of male pronouns when referring to the homework-trapped child) affect boys. It may not be the old nursery rhyme (i.e., "What are little boys made of? Snakes and snails and puppy dog tails. What are little girls made of? Sugar and spice and everything nice"). But it is often true that boys have better gross-motor skills (making them stronger at athletics), whereas girls have better fine-motor skills (giving them better handwriting skills). The mechanics of homework are simply easier for girls than they are for boys. So consequently, girls behave better in school.

Think about the work you do, whatever it is—being a secretary, a carpenter, a police officer, anything. You have work hours, maybe 9:00 to 5:00, or something else. You have co-workers. It is inconceivable that you and your co-workers produce at an identical pace. Yet, you all check in and check out at the same time. If you are particularly proficient, you may be in line for advancements that others are not going to get, just as an accelerated student may be heading for honors classes and academic accolades later on. If you are particularly slow, it is possible you might lose your job. Or, perhaps there is something else you can do where you are more proficient, and you should consider changing your field. Regardless, differences in performance speed do not usually force you to have to work longer without additional pay. Otherwise, your employer would be in violation of federal labor laws.

Without caps on time, differences in processing speed (and handwriting in particular) have a huge impact on the difficulties of children with chronic homework problems. The problem is not as pronounced in school, where every child attends for the same amount of time. At home, the slower the child processes information and outputs the results, the longer the actual homework session must be. Add on a common practice of having the child take home work to complete that he did not finish in class, and the impact is huge.

Contrary to common beliefs, the child in elementary school who is acknowledged and rewarded for being a good student in class will likely emerge as proficient at the high school and college levels, more than the one who works diligently at home. It is not training to do homework that causes the first child to excel. It is constant recognition and reinforcement for being a bright and accelerated student.

For the child in the middle of the processing-speed range, the one who has to do his homework in order to succeed, the system is not bad. Even though the truly gifted student actually gets a pass at the younger ages from having to work at home, the middle-range student can handle those assignments and proceed well with what he is required to do. For the slow-processing child, homework is a nightmare, which could be corrected by putting the assignments into a container defined by time, not just by what was assigned.

Although I place great emphasis on the problem of handwriting, there are other aspects of processing speed that can contribute to a child's homework problems. Reading speed is one, although its impact may have more bearing on the upper grades. Furthermore, chronic homework problems that start with slow processing speed have a cumulative effect on the acquisition of information and the child's overall emotional state. The less the child already knows, the more work is entailed in completing the assignments. The more pressure the child has felt, over the years, to get the work done, the more emotional factors (like anxiety, anger, and depression) come into play. Since the expectations move up as the child proceeds through advancing grades, that child hits a point where he finally shuts down, with serious consequences for his middle and high school work.

I have a general formula for responding to the problems of processing speed, if it affects your child. First, you need to establish fixed work hours, no more than ten minutes a night per grade. Second, you need to modify the penalties, so they don't end up being so severe that the child fails or that you, the parent, get too stressed out. Third, you need to take an educational approach to the processing-speed problem. This may mean occupational therapy for your child. It may mean that the school provides extra instruction in handwriting, reading, or whatever else the problem may be. You may choose to seek outside help on your own (perhaps a private tutor or learning center), although I caution you to be careful about burdening your child with too much school (e.g., have the child's homework waived the day he goes to the learning center, unless the tutor or teacher is actually having him do the work there).

A Special Note on ADHD

As noted before, there is great similarity between the concepts of working memory and attention. Children with poor working memory get bored and look inattentive, because they feel overloaded with more information than they can absorb. There are other children, however, who have primary problems with sustaining their attention. They're easily distracted, their minds wander, and they are often seen looking around rather than looking at the teacher or focusing on the task. They may also be hyperactive (e.g., fidgeting in their seats or getting up without permission and walking around). Sometimes, the fidgeting behavior is an act of brain stimulation that actually helps, rather than prevents that child from focusing on the task (much the way adults may stimulate attention by drinking that extra cup of coffee). Furthermore, these children can be impulsive, butting in while someone is talking and engaging in risky and dangerous behaviors.

If your child has ADHD, it is possible that you have consulted with his doctor and put him on a psychostimulant medication, such as Ritalin or Adderall. These medications can be quite effective in reducing hyperactive behaviors and in helping the child focus his attention. They are short-acting drugs, effective for anywhere from three to eight hours. Your child can easily be covered through the hours of school. What happens when he comes home?

Some children receive an afterschool dose of their medication. Some take something else, a non-stimulant, at night to supplement the morning meds. Some simply have no afterschool medication at all. Regardless of the plan for any particular child, it is important to understand that there are no solutions to medicating your child in the afternoon or at night that are as effective as what you can give him to cover his day.

Psychostimulant medications are generally safe, but they do affect both appetite and sleep. If you medicate him in the afternoon, it will probably interfere at dinnertime. He may get hungry late at night, causing him to stay up later than you think he should. Further, the fact that he has managed his behavior through the school day does not mean that he's ready to sit down and do his homework, after pulling through an entire day of school. He may simply need to blow off some steam. He may need a break to run around and play.

Yet, if you wait for the evening, it is highly likely that you are pushing him to work during his unmedicated state. If anything, his daytime medication may end up contributing to the notion that he can really do the work, without consideration for the fact that he's truly in a different mental (i.e., medicated) state when he is at home. This may force you to press him to work, under conditions that are grossly different from what they are at school, into the evening, without downtime, expecting him then to go right to sleep. It usually doesn't work. If your child requires medication, I'm sure I'm telling you nothing new. I'm just giving you a perspective for your own perceptions. Yet, I have rarely seen this factored in when considering what an ADHD child can do.

Interestingly, one of the accommodations that schools commonly give to ADHD children is extra time. You'll have very little difficulty getting the school, through the child study team, to agree to this simple modification. Think about it. More time, not less work. What does that mean?

In school, more time generally means a redistribution of the time, which is already there. The child goes to school 9:00 to 3:00. Perhaps he takes a math test during one of his periods, from 10:00 to 11:00. So he gets an extra half hour, and he continues the test from 11:00 to 11:30, passing on whatever else is scheduled then. That's not more time in school, but rather a shift in the allocation of time. Perhaps, more time means he'll continue his work through recess or through the lunch break. Here, the time is contained in the school day without interfering with other academic tasks. But what does that mean? Less time to renew himself and prepare for the rest of the day. Less time with friends, perhaps interfering with the acquisition of social skills. Isn't there a reason for recess? Isn't there a reason we give the children a half hour to eat, rather than have them gobble down their food while taking their tests? If the child has ADHD, he may need these release points even more than the average student his age, yet that's where we often take the extra time from.

But let's assume that giving more time, during school hours, is a reasonable accommodation for the ADHD child. At least it is time taken from the teacher's watch. I generally support giving teachers and the school the authority to make decisions when the child is in school. If they think the child will benefit from spending a little more time completing the assignment he is on, rather than getting pushed right into the lesson that comes next, I'm all for that. It might help.

But at home, where does the time come from? Don't you want your child to eat dinner, play a game, do a puzzle, read a book, watch some TV, spend time with his friends, take a bath, brush his teeth, sit with the family, and go to sleep? And don't you want to have the final authority to guide your child and make those decisions on his behalf? Without limits on the time your child spends doing homework, extra time only means spending more time, struggling over things he has trouble accomplishing and hates to do, without much tangible educational benefit involved.

I've talked a lot throughout this book about the value of placing limits on your child's homework time. Now, I'm going to modify that statement and say that it is possible that your ADHD child's homework accommodation may actually require that he spend *less time*. If your child has struggled to sustain his attention during the day, he needs to run and play when he gets home. He needs to unwind. You cannot adequately medicate him at night. Perhaps, he needs that time off as well. Perhaps, he needs a reduced assignment, so he can still be responsible, like all the other children, to do some work at home, yet only to the limits of what he can tolerate and do. His reasonable accommodation should be *more time* at school, *less time* at home.

Let's look at the pure mathematics of the situation. If your child is in fourth grade, where forty minutes of homework is considered the standard, and school is scheduled for six hours a day, that's 6X60+40 (it's okay if you have poor working memory, you can use paper and pencil if you like), or four hundred minutes a day, of which only forty should be done at home. Ninety percent of his educational time takes place in school! What would it mean for him to be required to work half the expected time (i.e., twenty minutes a night)? That's only a 5 percent reduction in his total academic time. Yet, we routinely take children who have this condition and make them sit over books for hours every night. It is not fair, and even more important, it does not work.

7. WHAT to DO

Now that you understand what is going on, you need to decide what you are going to do. You have three basic levels on which to work. You can make changes in your home, independent of what the teachers do. You can seek changes with your child's teachers and the school. You can talk with other parents to rally support for system-wide recognition of the need to think differently about homework, in general, and for children with chronic homework problems, in particular. I'll review your options for each approach.

In Your Home

Your first and most important step is to fully assume your role as *head of your home.* You must embrace the concept that you are in charge and have the right to establish, in your home, the norms in which you believe. You do that in every other area of your child's life, such as religious training, sports participation, piano lessons, family vacations, relationships with relatives, dinner rituals, and the list goes on. In each case, what you do reflects your values and beliefs. You may not run your home the way other people do. Who knows? Maybe your approach is better. Maybe it is not. It does not matter. This is what it means to be the head of your home. The simple act of taking this common-sense notion, and applying it to the expectations you set in your home regarding homework, immediately gives you greater authority with your child than you had before. Right now, you may feel like an agent, working for the school. You may have been engaged in parent-teacher meetings, which are intended to help your child improve, yet they end up diminishing your authority. You may have been placed in a position of responsibility without authority, and that's a dead end when it comes to being an effective parent. First and foremost, own the role of head of the home. Your child needs to understand that he is dealing with you and the rules you set in your home, not dictates coming from school.

Second, you need to establish *time-based rules* for your child's homework time. He needs to know when homework time starts and when it stops, just like he knows when his school day starts and stops. Ask yourself how much time you think a child his age should spend on educational tasks. Seven hours? Seven and a half hours? Eight hours? More? Consider your job and the job his other parent has. How much time do you each spend at work? If that amount is reasonable for an adult, what do you think is reasonable and fair for a person your child's age? Once you have a number, subtract the amount of time he spends in school (I assume it is about six hours), and that gives you a possible standard for what you expect him to do.

Alternatively, use the Harris Cooper standard of ten minutes per night per grade. Ten minutes for first grade, twenty for second grade, you get the idea. Or, ask the teachers during Back to School Night how much time they expect your child to work. Write those numbers down and decide if the total makes sense to you. If it does, use that as a basis for determining how much work your child must do.

Third, *control the environment.* Turn the TV off. Prohibit cell phone use. Restrict the computer only to its use as a tool for getting homework done (e.g., researching materials on the internet, or as a word processor).

Fourth, *identify the exact times* of day (try to keep it consistent) when homework will be done. You can discuss your decisions with your child, and even give him some room to negotiate with you. But in the end, tie the notions of the quiet environment, fixed time frames, and agreed-upon homework hours together, so he understands he's not entering the abyss of unending work, but a limited time/space frame in which to comply. He may have resisted your efforts in the past, but remember, you are giving him a big incentive to cooperate (i.e., that homework time will come to an end).

Fifth, *alter your interactions* with your child. Say the H-word at most twice a day, when homework starts and when homework stops. Say the word with neutral affect, and in a matter-of-fact tone. Don't fight, and if you do fight, don't use the word "homework" during the argument.

Sixth, *emphasize the positives.* Keep in mind that shaping is needed to undo negative behaviors, and that involves rewards for small efforts and partial success. If you have something critical or negative to say, adopt the four-to-one rule, which means four positive statements for every critical one made.

Seventh, *model* academic behavior. Read a book, perhaps in the room where he does his work. Make yourself available without hovering over or monitoring what he does.

Eighth, be an *observer*, not an enforcer. Make mental notes (whether you are in the room with him, or periodically passing by) of what he is doing, and what problems he seems to have. Try to understand the particular reason why your child may be having problems with the work.

Ninth, consider the issue *educational*, not moral or behavioral. Think about what problems of learning may be contributing to his homework difficulties. In particular, pay attention to signs of problems with working memory (e.g., lapsed attention) and processing speed (e.g., poor handwriting or slow reading skills).

Tenth, *preserve your family.* Remember, the family is there to protect its members and help them refuel for the next day. I doubt that you expect your partner or spouse to get on your case when you come home to continue working at your job. You expect respite, a time to unwind, and some feeling of relief. Your child deserves that too. Tenaciously hold onto the qualitative factors you want and enjoy in your home.

These are steps you can take in your home, whether or not the school is on board, whether or not they are willing to make changes.

With the School

You may have already discussed your child's homework problems with the school. Most likely, the energy seems to move from the school to you, not the other way around. The homework requirement is considered sacrosanct. Changes are to take place mostly in your home. There is usually very little discussion of the changes you want the school to make. Let's make this a two-way street.

First, share with them your belief that this is a *problem of learning*, not just one of behavior or motivation. Be prepared to identify the specific difficulties you feel your child is having with the work.

Second, seek *educational solutions* to the problems you observe. If it's working memory, highlight your concern that he is not absorbing what is said in school. If they say he is not paying attention, seek solutions that capitalize on the attention he displays, not the attention they think he should display. If you think his handwriting is the problem, ask for the involvement of an occupational therapist. If it's reading, ask if they can teach him to increase his reading speed. If they recommend that you secure that on your own from an outside learning center (whether for reading speed, extra help in math, or so on), consider the possibility, if you think you can, but think of it in lieu of, not added on, to what he does.

Third, discuss *bypass strategies*. If you child does not write well, seek alternative ways of testing what he knows or getting his homework done (e.g., dictation, word processing), until he has developed the needed handwriting skill. Ask that assignments be given in written as well as verbal form (that does not mean put on the board for him to write down, particularly if he has a handwriting problem).

Fourth, inform the school of your *time-based decision*. This is matter-of-fact, no negotiations involved. Remind them of the estimates they shared when you asked them at Back to School Night, and explain how you arrived at the standard you use. Let them know that your child has a time-bound educational day, and that you'll work with them to figure out ways to use that time well.

Fifth, request *modified grades*. Your child needs modified grades, so he can experience reinforcement and success for the work he does within his designated homework times. Further, you need modified grades, so you can approach his problem with calmness, rather than panic. There are several models for grade modification you can request. They include the following:

1. Full credit, without penalties for work not done, according to your rules. You agree to certify that he worked the requisite hours. The teacher agrees not to lower his grade for work not done.

2. Failure floor. With this model, zeros for work not done get recalculated as sixties in the final grade. This limits the effect of an assignment not done to that of an ordinary failing grade.

3. Recalibrated grading system. Here, homework contributes to no more than 10 percent of your child's marking-period grade. For example, if his teacher ordinarily counts 25 percent of the grade for tests, quizzes, classroom participation, and homework, he or she now calculates your child's grade as 33 percent for tests, quizzes, and classroom participation, but only 10 percent for homework. Ask for a limit to the degree to which homework can pull down his final score. Ask that his grade not be diminished by more than a half- to a full-letter grade, based on the impact homework has.

Finally, there are some special considerations based on what grade your child is in. If you are fortunate enough to institute these ideas while he is in elementary school, the following concept does not apply. If, like many parents with homework-trapped children, your child is already in middle or high school, you have to consider that he has several major teachers, all with their own homework requirements. For that, you need to consider how to balance the influx of multiple demands. You also need a simple mechanism by which you can communicate with the school (i.e., you want to avoid holding separate discussions with each of his teachers). For this, you need an identified contact from the school, most desirably in the form of a study-skills teacher. Here is how it works.

The study-skills teacher oversees a study-skills class that is offered to your child in lieu of his regular study-hall time. In that class, the teacher will do the following:

1. Monitor your child's work.
2. Identify sources of educational need, related to effective homework completion, and help him become better at the task.
3. Communicate with his teachers regarding homework priorities, knowing that his actual homework time is limited to what you've designated for him at home and the time he spends in study-skills class.
4. Help your child prioritize his work.
5. Serve as your primary contact person with the school.

This model can be used in both middle and high school, although there are some differences to consider in high school.

First, there are more levels to select from in high school courses—basic, regular, honors, and AP. Typically, choices are made based on your child's academic potential, not based on how much work he'll have to do. Seek accurate estimates of the homework time needed at each level, and use that in determining what courses he takes.

Second, keep in mind how important high school life is to personal and social development. Extracurricular activities are not just a reward for good behavior and secondary to academic success. They are vital to the child's health and welfare. Even if it is reasonable to expect more work at this level, it is essential to ensure that your child does not lose access to school-based activities.

The Community at Large

I've spoken to countless parents and teachers about the homework problem. I have never encountered a teacher who does not have at least one homework-trapped child in his or her class. I talk to parents who have three or four children, and inevitably they have one who is homework trapped. The problem is massive. Yet, people hide in shame. They do not talk openly about the problems their children are having. If it is just yours, it seems like a specific and unique problem. If the numbers get accurately counted, it is clearly an educational phenomenon of considerable importance that the school has failed to handle well.

Yet, chronic homework noncompliance is also a problem that is hard to understand, if you are not having it in your own home. Just as there are parents whose children desperately require homework relief, there are other parents whose children have no difficulty with the work they get, and some who believe their children should get more. Perhaps, those are the ones who are speaking out. Maybe, they're the ones who head the local PTA. Maybe, they are the ones the teachers keep in mind, in assuring themselves that their policies make sense and their requirements are fair. Without a voice, the homework-trapped child's problem will only be discussed in school-teacher meetings, where the focus may be on you, your child, and what may be wrong *in your home.* You may be perceived as defensive and unable to clearly see *the truth* about your child, without true consideration of how the expectations and demands are contributing to the problem. I mentioned at the beginning of this book that I have three children, one of whom had severe homework problems. Frankly, as a psychologist, I have had much greater success explaining these points when talking to educational and community groups than I had when sitting at a meeting in my own child's school, talking about my own kid. You, too, will have more success if you can raise the discussion to a community-wide level, rather than being limited to your child alone.

There's a little-known fact about homework policy, which is that teachers are not trained in the art of giving homework. To the best of my knowledge, no school of education has a course (or major section of an educational course) devoted to the topic of how to use homework. Teachers are left to their own devices in incorporating this component. Just think about your child's experience. Wasn't it somewhat different, during elementary school, from year to year, depending on which teacher your child had? They are not uniform or fully consistent in how they assign, grade, and factor in the homework that they give. Didn't things get worse (if your child is at this stage) once he entered middle school? This is because among any group of independently minded teachers, there will be variations in the expectations and policies they have. As soon as you have multiple teachers, you are going to have disparate and conflicting demands. For the child who has not experienced tranquility and success at the elementary school level, it is too hard to comply.

If you can create a subgroup of parents with similar problems who are not ashamed, and who are able to speak boldly and openly, not simply complain but jointly subscribe to the philosophies and plans I've described, your chances increase. And since there is not a common, uniformly agreed-upon, policy and practice for incorporating homework into the educational process, you have a basis to ask that the teachers and the schools educate themselves and incorporate, into policy, the types of information found in this book (and found in other books that experts and critics in the homework field have written).

Most schools have some in-service training program for their teachers to increase their professional skills. Most state teacher's associations have regular conferences geared toward providing continued education and training for them. Start a parent-centered push for your child's school to adopt a system-wide approach to the problem of homework difficulties.

8. CONCLUSION

I n summarizing this book, I will review the main concepts we have covered.

Chronic homework noncompliance is an educational, not a behavioral problem. Bad behavior is an adaptive response to ongoing pressures to get work done that the child cannot do. Parent-teacher efforts to coordinate their response serve to reinforce, not diminish, acting-out behavior. While there may be some children who give positive responses to the plans parents and teachers make together, it is often the case that these are simply different children, not the ones who are chronically homework trapped.

For the homework-trapped child, the problem is cumulative, getting worse year after year. This child is particularly unprepared for the complexities he'll face in middle school, when he'll have multiple teachers. By high school, this child faces true risks of turning away from school and seeking peer groups that are not good for him. Meanwhile, homework demands are actually interfering with other educational activities the child could pursue on his own at home (e.g., art, mechanics, construction, athletics, and healthy play).

The concept of classical conditioning tells us that homework resistance becomes an automatic response that needs to be deconditioned through a different way of talking about the task. The concept of operant conditioning tells us that avoidance is a learned response, and that the homework-trapped child needs the shaping of positive homework behavior, which essentially means full credit for partial success. The concept of modeling tells us that we need to capitalize on positive relationships between the parent and the child, including the parent's capacity to model productive behaviors. Maturation is a developmental process that suggests that pressure to comply may actually interfere with an innate tendency for the child to grow up and mature out of the problem.

I discussed the complicated relationships between the school and family systems, and how clarity in roles is critically important for your child's health and success. In school, the teachers are in charge of what goes on. You are in charge of what happens in your home. Assignment of work in your home, with the power to penalize beyond your control, sets off a dysfunctional dynamic that inevitably works against homework success.

There is a common-sense notion that children, like adults, work best during fixed periods of times. Adults have work hours. Children need them, too. School, in fact, has designated school hours and classroom periods of time. Such time frames need to occur in your home as well.

Teachers form opinions of children based on what they see when the child is in class. There they see both the product of the child's work, and the process by which the child gets the work done. Homework takes place at a different hour of the day, with the teacher only privy to the product, not the process. It is not rational to draw implications about a child's capacity to work, at home at night, from what he can do during the day in school.

The parents' most effective role with regard to their children's homework is that of an observer, not an enforcer. Parents can provide valuable information for professional teachers to employ in their craft, as long as they are not driven beyond reason to make sure everything gets done. They are the eyes and ears of the child's homework process, and this can contribute to his educational development. It is essential that they do this without excessive fears that their children will fail if tonight's assignment is not done.

All roads lead to a simple formula that includes time-based assignments, modifications of the assignments so they are doable within the designated times, and modifications of the penalty structure as well. There needs to be a focus on identifying the *under-the-radar* learning problems, with a combination of remediation and bypass strategy training. In the end, we should not throw out the *baby with the bathwater* (i.e., let the child who can learn and succeed fail simply because he does not comply).

The parent can take steps in his or her own home alone. The parent can interact with the school, with the expectation of accommodations so the child can succeed. The parent can open dialogue with the school community at large, with the hopes of causing the changes he or she needs and of garnering widespread acceptance of a new model for homework-trapped children, rather than remaining isolated and frustrated in a battle for his or her child alone.

·REFERENCES·

Bandura, A. (1977). *Social Learning Theory.* Englewood Cliffs, NJ, Prentice Hall.

Bennett, S., & Kalish, N. (2006). *The Case Against Homework: How Homework Is Hurting Our Children and What We Can Do About It.* New York, Crown Publishers.

Cooper, H. (2001). *The Battle over Homework: Common Ground for Administrators, Teachers, and Parents.* Thousand Oaks, CA, Corwin Press.

Dolin, A. (2010). *Homework Made Simple: Tips, Tools, and Solutions for Stress-free Homework.* Washington, Advantage Books.

Hu, W. "New Recruit in Homework Revolt: The Principal," *The New York Times,* June 15, 2011.

Kohn. A. (2006). *The Homework Myth: Why Our Kids Get Too Much of a Bad Thing.* Cambridge, MA, Da Capo Press.

Kralovec, E. (2007). "A Brief History of Homework." *Encounter: Education for Meaning and Social Justice.* 20(4), 8-12.

Kralovec, E. & Buell, J. (2000). *The End of Homework: How Homework Disrupts Families, Overburdens Children, and Limits Learning.* Boston, Beacon Press.

Pavlov, I. P. (1927). *Conditioned Reflexes: An Investigation of the Physiological Activity of the Cerebral Cortex* (translated by G. V. Anrep). London, Oxford University Press.

Rosemond, J. (1990). *Ending the Homework Hassle.* Riverside, NJ, Andrews McMeel.

Skinner, B.F. (1938). *The Behavior of Organisms:An Experimental Analysis.* Cambridge, MA, Copley Publishing Group.

Vatterott, C. (2009). *Rethinking Homework: Best Practices that Support Diverse Needs.* Alexandria, VA, ASCD.

Wechsler, D. (2003). *Wechsler Intelligence Scale for Children—Fourth Edition.* San Antonio, TX, Pearson.

·APPENDIX·

How do you know if you and your child are homework trapped? Ask yourself these.

Does your child have the following characteristics:

- My child won't complete his homework.

- My child will endure almost any punishment rather than complete his homework.

- Even when my child tries to do his homework, very little actually gets done.

- My child refuses my help with homework assignments.

- Homework assignments rarely make it from school to home.

- Homework that is done rarely makes it from home to school.

- Even if the homework gets to school, it's rarely handed in.

- Other than homework, my child does fairly well at school.

- When my child first started, he was eager and truly enjoyed school.

- My child has very poor handwriting.

If these statements describe your child, he may be homework-trapped. Do you have the following experiences?

- I think about my child's homework much of the time.

- I talk about homework many times each night.

- I shudder at the thought of asking my child if he has homework or if his homework has been done.

- I speak with the teachers more than I want, and I never feel good when those meetings are done.

- I've joined my child's teachers in constructing plans that never work to solve the homework problem.

- Homework seems the most important issue in my child's life.

- I've lost authority over my child in other areas that matter to me.

If these statements characterize your home life, you may be homework-trapped.

·ACKNOWLEDGEMENTS·

There are many people to whom I am grateful. They have contributed to *The Homework Trap* in ways large and small, knowingly and unwittingly. I'll start by mentioning the hundreds, perhaps thousands, of people who helped with this book but were unaware of their role. Over the years, I have administered many IQ tests to adults and to children. It is through these tests that I observed a pattern of strengths and weaknesses that consistently predicted (or reflected) chronic homework problems. Following such test administrations, I often talked with my clients and, over time, began sharing the ideas that are found in this book. It was that look of understanding and agreement with my ideas that helped me develop these concepts. Over time, I developed my ten-minute elevator speech, a synopsis of what was actually going on with kids who spend hours fighting with their parents, struggling with their assignments, and feeling ashamed in front of their teachers, yet over the years, have nothing to show for it. It was that look of understanding, that constant confirmation, that propelled me to write this book. I am forever grateful for the privilege of meeting so many people, strangers, with whom I could share my perceptions and formulate my ideas.

There are several individuals who played specific, personal roles and deserve credit for helping me with this book. First, there is Joyce Faulkner, my friend and fellow writer. Joyce was instrumental early on, supporting me in writing this book. She played a substantial part in convincing me that I could publish it on my own, simply because I had something to say. Jay Kuder, professor of education and chair of the Department of Special Education at Rowan University, was my partner through the early stages of my work. Jay joined me in developing ideas and presenting them to the public. Jay played a crucial role, as a friend and as an educator (after all, I'm a psychologist not a teacher), in acquainting me with the educational side of the picture. Etta Kralovec, professor of education at the University of Arizona and co-author of *The End of Homework: How Homework Disrupts Families, Overburdens Children, and Limits Learning*, deserves credit as well. Etta showed confidence in me at an early stage in developing my thoughts. Although I was relatively unknown, she invited me to join a panel addressing homework problems at the American Educational Research Association's annual conference. Her support proved crucial for me to later move on and produce this book. I want to thank my wife, Maryka, who has always believed in me and who has always been my editor *par excellence*. Maryka reviews and makes comments on everything that I write, incisively contributing to both content and style. I thank my children, Matt, Sasha, and BB, who tolerated my learning on the job to become a good parent, including their lessons on children doing homework. I appreciate their specific help with website design and showing me how to do social networking. There were others who helped both in the production and promotion of this book. I thank Meg Schultz for her exceptional artistic skills in providing the illustrations as well as the cover design. I thank Susan Carroll, who advised me in a variety of aspects as to producing and presenting this book. My friend, Steve Sharp, a professional photographer, took the pictures for my website and the cover of this book. I thank the staff at Smith Publicity for helping me reach out to the public with my homework message. Finally, I appreciate the work of the CreateSpace staff. They are an excellent organization that makes it possible for authors like me to publish a quality book on their own.

·ABOUT the AUTHOR·

Kenneth Goldberg is a clinical psychologist with more than thirty years of professional experience in dealing with many different psychological issues, in both in-patient and out-patient settings. Through his career, he has served children, adolescents, and adults, offering individual and group psychotherapy, as well as marriage and family counseling. Prior to starting his private practice, Dr. Goldberg served as clinical director for a children's residential treatment facility, as director of a psychiatric day-treatment program for the chronically mentally ill, and as the head of a rural mental-health center. He has been a frequent speaker and consultant on programs designed to serve psychiatric populations. His first book, *Differing Approaches for Partial Hospitalization* (1988), was an edited volume comparing treatment modalities in community-based programs for people who are chronically mentally ill.

A member of the American Psychological Association, Dr. Goldberg currently conducts psychological evaluations for disabled workers and for those accused by the state of harming their children. Dr. Goldberg's interest in persistent homework problems was stimulated not just by his personal experience and his work with children, but through studies conducted with disabled adults. Unlike those who work primarily with children, Dr. Goldberg understands the long-term effects that chronic homework problems have on people later in life, as adults and in their roles as parents.

Prior to becoming a psychologist, Dr. Goldberg was a mathematician. He attended Columbia University on a National Science Foundation Scholarship and as a Woodrow Wilson Fellow. He left Columbia with a master's degree in math and went on to Long Island University, where he earned a PhD in clinical psychology. Dr. Goldberg brings his mathematical way of thinking to his clinical work, enabling him to see patterns of behavior in unique ways.

Dr. Goldberg has also dabbled with literary fiction and is the author of *Peter Squared*, which was published by Macadam Cage in 2000. Dr. Goldberg's next project, after completing his work on *The Homework Trap*, will be to publish *Peter Cubed*, the sequel to his first novel. Dr. Goldberg is the proud father of three adult children (all of whom have had different homework experiences) and is married to Maryka Matthews, a retired psychiatric social worker. In his free time, Dr. Goldberg enjoys tennis, chess and Scrabble™ (and although he does not feel trapped, he often does work at home).

Dr. Goldberg can be contacted through one of his websites: www.thehomeworkdoctor.com or www.drkengoldberg.com.

·NOTES·

·NOTES·

·NOTES·

·NOTES·

·NOTES·

Made in the USA
Lexington, KY
10 October 2012